Every Girl is Born a Queen

Queen Ari Allah

To order additional copies of this book, contact:
Xlibris
844-714-8691
www.Xlibris.com
Orders@Xlibris.com

ISBN: Softcover   978-1-6641-6830-5
         EBook   978-1-6641-6829-9

Print information available on the last page

Rev. date: 02/11/2022

I dedicate this book to my perfect little sister, MyJustice. She's the cutest little Queen I've ever seen. And to my beautiful cousins and God sisters, Shay, Fantasia, Karis, Happi, Logan, Nylah, Kiki, Emani, Aoki, Sanai, Milan and Samaya. Thank you girls for always having my back and reminding me how important it is to help each other's crowns from slipping. I love and appreciate all of you.

Every girl is born a Queen!

She's crowned before she's even seen.

A Queen of life.

A Queen of love.

A Queen of kisses.

And a Queen of hugs.

She's the Queen of crying.

And a Queen of smiling.

The Queen of fun with the coolest toys.

She's a cute little Queen
who brings so much joy.

Printed in the United States
by Baker & Taylor Publisher Services